GW00836294

NEWTOWN
TO
ABERYSTWYTH

Vic Mitchell and Keith Smith

MP Middleton Press

Front cover: No. 7819 Hinton Manor *leaves Dovey Junction with the up "Cambrian Coast Express" on 3rd June 1963. The bridge over the River Dovey for the Pwllheli line is on the right. The locomotive has subsequently worked on the Severn Valley Railway. (T.J.Edgington)*

Back cover: Unit no. 158848 waits to leave Aberystwyth as the 13.15 to Birmingham New Street on 21st May 2004. (P.Jones)

Published December 2008

ISBN 978 1 906008 41 3

© *Middleton Press, 2008*

Design Deborah Esher
Typesetting Barbara Mitchell

Published by
    Middleton Press
    Easebourne Lane
    Midhurst
    West Sussex
    GU29 9AZ
Tel: 01730 813169
Fax: 01730 812601
Email: info@middletonpress.co.uk
www.middletonpress.co.uk

Printed & bound by Biddles Ltd, Kings Lynn

INDEX

ACKNOWLEDGEMENTS

We are very grateful for the assistance received from many of those mentioned in the credits, also to A.R.Carder, L.Crosier, G.Croughton, F.Hornby, J.B.Horne, N.Langridge, B.Lewis, D.H.Mitchell, B.I.Nathan, A.Rhodes, Mr D. and Dr S.Salter, M.Turvey, T.Walsh and, in particular, our always supportive wives Barbara Mitchell and Janet Smith.

I. Railway Clearing House map with minor additions.

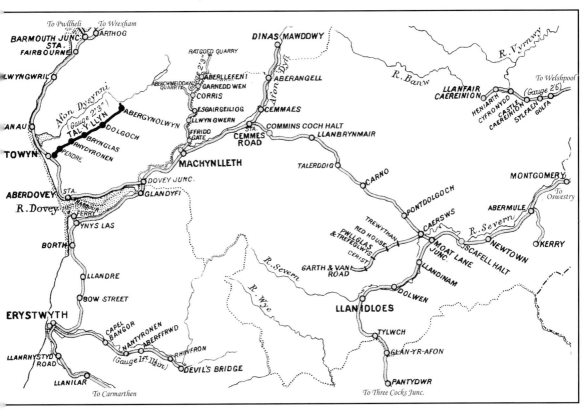

GEOGRAPHICAL SETTING

Newtown is a market town, which once had extensive wool manufacturing facilities. It is in the upper part of the Severn Valley and the route follows this river upstream to Caersws. The Van Railway branched south here to serve mines producing lead, zinc and some silver.

The main line's gentle climb becomes severe for eight miles to the summit at Talerddig, where it crosses the Cambrian Mountains. The descent is at an even steeper gradient and it enters the Dovey Valley at Cemmes Road. Running up the valley from here was the Dinas Mawddwy branch, this serving a great wool producing district. We continue down the valley to Machynlleth, once the seat of power in Wales under Prince Owain Glyndwr.

The valley broadens greatly westwards, Machynlleth being the lowest crossing point of the River Dovey by road. However, the Cambrian Coast lines diverge more than three miles nearer the sea, at Dovey Junction.

Most of the route is over sandstones and the final section is particularly undulating. We travel from Powys to Ceredigion, the boundary being just south of Dovey Junction. Until 1974,

WHITCHURCH, OSWESTRY, WELSHPOOL, and ABERYSTWYTH.

Miles from Whitchurch	Down. Week Days.	aft	mrn	mrn	mrn	mrn	mrn	mrn	mrn	aft	aft
							Mondays only.	Birkenhead and Manchester (London Road) to Aberystwyth.	Wednesdays and Saturdays.	Saturdays; and last Tuesday in each month only.	Saturdays only.
	488 London (Euston) ....dep.	10 50				2 35					
	488 Manchester (Ln. Rd.) "	11 45				6 0		8 35			
	488 Liverpool (Lime St.) "	11D50				2 30		8 15			
	488 Crewe .... "	2 5				7 34		9 25			
—	Whitchurch ....dep.	2 45				8 17		10 0			
3	Fenn's Bank					8 23		10 7			
6¾	Bettisfield					8 31		10 15			
7¾	Welshampton					8 34		10 19			
10¾	Ellesmere 129	3 7				8 43		10 26			
12¾	Frankton ....[108, 112					8 48		10 31			
16¼	Whittington (High Level)					8 56		10 40			
18¼	Oswestry 94, 137 ......arr.	3 20				9 0		10 44			
—	108 London (Paddington) dep.						1 30	1 30	9 10		
—	112 Manchester (Exch.). "	10X20					5 50	7 20	9 40		
—	112 Liverpool (LandgStg) "	11X15			6 15		7 40	8 50	9 50		
—	112 Birkenhead (W'side) "	11X33			6 30		8 0	9 5	10 3		
—	112 Chester (General) ... "	12X20			7 8		8 35	9 40	11 5		
—	Oswestry ....dep.	3 30		7 50	8 20		9 35	10 55	1 0		
22	Llynclys			7 57			9 42	11 2	1 7		
23¼	Pant (Salop)			8 0			9 45	11 5	1 10		
24¼	Llanymynech 129 ......arr.	3 40		8 3	8 29		9 47	11 8	1 12		
32¾	129 Llanfyllin ....arr.			Stop	8 56			11 36	1 35		
—	Llanymynech ....dep.	3 42			8 30		9 48	11 10			
25¾	Four Crosses				8 33		9 52	11 14			
27¼	Arddleen				8 38		9 56				
29¼	Pool Quay				8 43		10 0	11 22			
31¼	Buttington 487				8 48		10 5	11 27			
33¾	Welshpool ....arr.	4 0			8 54		1010	11 32			
—	108 London (Paddington) dep.				1 30						
—	487 " (Euston) .... "	9H25			2j35			2 35			
—	108 Birmingham (Snow H.) "				6 0			8 33			
—	487 " (New St.) "	10H45			2j35			7 15			
—	Mls Shrewsbury (Gen.) ..dep.	3 25			7 55			10 27			
—	4¾ Hanwood				8 4			10 36			
—	7½ Yockleton				8 10			10 42			
—	11 Westbury ¶				8 21			10 52			
—	14 Breidden				8 30			11 1			
—	17 Buttington 144				8 36			11 7			
—	19¾ Welshpool ....arr.	4 3			8 42			11 13			
—	Welshpool ....dep.	4 15			9 0			11 38			
38¼	Forden				9 8			11 45			
40	Montgomery A	4 26			9 12			11 50			
44	Abermule				9 21			11 58			
47¾	Newtown	4 42			9 28			12 13		2 20	
52¼	Moat Lane Junction 150 arr.	4 55			9 37			12 22		2 27	
59¾	150 Llanidloes ....arr.	5 29			10 11			12Y43		2 51	
112¼	150 Brecon .... "	8 5			12 24			5 8		5 8	
—	Moat Lane Junction ....dep.	5 0			9 42			TC 12 25			
53¼	Caersws	5 3			9 45			12 28			
55	Pontdolgoch				9 49			12 32			
59¼	Carno	5 16			9 57			12 41			
61¼	Talerddig				10 3			12 46			
64¾	Llanbrynmair ¶	5 27			10 10			12 53			
70	Cemmes Road B	5 37			10 20			1 4			
75	Machynlleth 146 .... arr.	5 45		mrn	10 29			1 15			
	dep.	5 53	6 10	8 15	10 31			1 17			3 24
79	Dovey Junction ....arr.			8 21	10 37			1 23			3 30
88½	146 Towyn ....arr.		6 39	8 56	11 20			2 2			3 59
100½	146 Barmouth .... "		7 9	9 26	11 51			2 34			4 44
132¾	146 Pwllheli .... "		8 59	1055	1 43			3 59			6 10
—	Dovey Junction ....dep.			8 38	10 44			1 25			3 34
79¾	Glandyfi	6 2		8 40	10 48			1 29			3 37
85¼	Ynyslas			8 50	10 58			1 41			3 47
87¼	Borth	6 14		8 54	11 4			1 44			3 51
89¾	Llandre	6 22		9 0	11 11			1 51			3 57
91¼	Bow Street	6 26		9 4	11 15			1 55			4 1
95¾	Aberystwyth 141 ......arr.	6 35		9 13	11 25			2 5			4 10

A Station nearly 2 miles from Montgomery.
B 1¾ miles from Cemmes.
D Departs Liverpool (Lime Street) at 10 45 aft. on Sundays.
F Except Mondays.
H Except Sunday nights.
j Mondays only.
TC Through Carriage
X Except Sundays. Via Shrewsbury. On Thursday nights via Oswestry.
Y One class only.
¶ "Halt" at Plas-y-Court between Westbury and Breidden and at Commins Coch, between Llanbrynmair and Cemmes Road

February 1936

we would have journeyed through Montgomeryshire to that location and then into Cardiganshire. The northern two stations of the Dinas Mawddwy branch were in Merionethshire. The maps are to the scale of 25ins to 1 mile, with north at the top unless otherwise indicated.

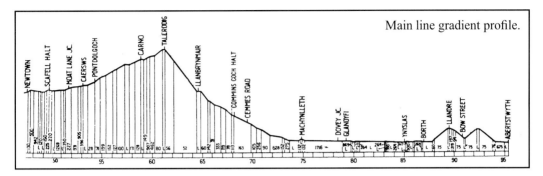

Main line gradient profile.

February 1936 continued

WHITCHURCH, OSWESTRY, WELSHPOOL, and ABERYSTWYTH.

Down.	Week Days—Continued.									Sundays.	
	mrn aft	aft	aft mrn aft	aft aft aft	aft aft aft		aft aft		aft mrn		
488London (Euston)....dep.	10 0 ..	..	1150	..	2 40	..	5 10	..	10 50	..
488Manchester (L. Rd.) ,,	12 9 ..	..	2 25	..	4 30	..	7 10	..	11 45	..
488Liverpool (Lime St.) ,,	12 0 ..	..	2 15	..	4V 0	..	7 5	..	11 50	..
488Crewe ,,	1 15 ..	..	3 27	..	5 50	..	8 17	..	2 5	..
Whitchurch ....dep.	1 50 2 5	..	4 5	..	6 50	..	9 0	..	2 40	..
Fenn's Bank	.. 2 12	..	4 11	..	6 57	..	9 7	..	..	..
Bettisfield	.. 2 19	..	4 19	..	7 5	..	9 15	..	..	..
Welshampton	.. 2 28	..	4 26	..	7 9	..	9 20	..	..	..
Ellesmere 129	2 13 2 36	..	4 34	..	7 18	..	9 38	..	3 8	..
Frankton.............[112	.. 2 41	..	4 39	..	7 23	..	9 43	..	..	..
Whittington (H. Level) 103,	.. 2 49	..	4 48	..	7 31	..	9 51	..	3 16	..
Oswestry 94, 137 .....arr.	2 26 2 53	..	4 53	..	7 36	..	9 55	..	3 20	..
108London (Pad.)....dep.	11 5	..	1120	..	2 10 .. 4 5	..	6 10	..	12710	..
112Manchester (Ex.).. ,,	12 5	..	1 45	..	3 38 5 32 6 40	..	6 40	..	10 20	..
112Liverpool (Ldg. S.) ,,	11840	..	1 0 2 20	..	4 20 6 0 7 0	..	7 0	..	11 15	..
112Birkenhead (W'side) ,,	11855	..	1 18 2 40	..	4 35 6 15 7 15	..	7 15	..	11 33	..
112Chester (General) .. ,,	1Y15	..	2 0 3 15	..	5 10 6 52 8 0	..	8 0	..	12720	..
Oswestry ....dep.	2 32 3 5	..	3 30 5 8	..	6 15 7 55 9 10	..	1110	..	6 15	..
Llynclys	.. 3 13	..	3 37 5 15	..	6 22 8 9 17	..	1117	..	mrn	..
Pant (Salop)	.. 3 16	..	3 40 5 18	..	6 25 8 9 20	..	1120	..	..	..
Llanymynech 129 .....arr.	.. 3 19	..	3 43 5 21	..	6 28 8 9 23	..	1123	..	6 25	..
129Llanfyllin ....arr.		..	4 7 5 48	..	6 53 .. 9 53	..	1148	..	..	..
Llanymynech ....dep.		..	5 22	..	8 9 9 25	..	..	..	6 26	..
Four Crosses	.. 3 23	..	Stop 5 25	..	8 13 9 28	..	..	..	6 30	..
Arddleen	.. 3 31	..	5 30	..	8 17	..	..	..	..	..
Pool Quay	.. 3 35	..	5 35	..	8 22 Stop	..	..	..	..	..
Buttington 487	.. 3 40	..	5 40	..	8 27	..	..	..	..	..
Welshpool .....arr.	2 57 3 43	..	5 45	..	8 32	..	..	..	6 45	..
108London (Paddington)dep.	11 C5	..	2N10	..	1 T 5	..	C710	..	12710	..
487 ,, (Euston)..... ,,	10 40	..	12 5	..	2 50	..	5 20	..	..	..
108Birmingham (SnowH) ,,	1C15	..	4N15	..	6T15	..	8N15	..	3J50	..
487 ,, (New Street) ,,	12 10	..	2 0	..	4 53	..	6 42	..	..	..
Shrewsbury (Gen.) ...dep.	2 30 3 5	..	5 30	..	7 35	..	9 38	..	5J13	..
Hanwood	.. 3 14	..	5 40	..		..	9 47	..	..	..
Yockleton	.. 3 20	..	5 47	..	7 49	..	9 54	..	..	..
Westbury ¶	.. 3 27	..	5 55	..	7 57	..	10 1	..	..	..
Breidden	.. 3 37	..	6 5	..	8	..	1013	..	..	..
Buttington 144	.. 2 44	..	6 10	..	Xx	..	1020	..	..	..
Welshpool ....arr.	3 5 3 50	..	6 16	..	8 17	..	1025	..	..	..
Welshpool...........dep.	3 12 4 0	..	6 21	..	8 34	..	..	..	6 48	..
Forden	.. 4 8	..	6 29	..	8 42	..	..	..	..	..
Montgomery A	Yy 4 12	..	6 34	..	8 47	..	..	..	7 0	..
Abermule	.. 4 23	..	6 42	..	8 53	..	..	..	7 8	..
Newtown	3 36 4 30	..	6 49	..	9 0	..	..	..	7 15	..
Moat Lane Junc. 150...arr.	3 44 4 40	..	6 57	..	9 8	..	..	..	..	..
150Llanidloes........arr.	4 11 5 8	..	8 11	..	9 26	..	..	..	..	..
150Brecon ,,	7 19	..	..	..	aft	..	..	..	..	..
Moat Lane Junction....dep.	3 47 4 44	..	7 0	..	9 11	..	..	..	7 27	..
Caersws	.. 4 48	..	7 3	..	9 14	..	..	..	..	..
Pontdolgoch	.. 4 52	..	7 8	..		..	..	..	7 41	..
Carno	.. 5 1	..	7 18	..		..	..	..	..	..
Talerddig	.. 5 13	..	7 23	..		..	..	..	7 54	..
Llanbrynmair ¶	.. 5 19	..	7 39	..		..	..	..	8 4	..
Cemmes Road B..	Yy 5 23	..	7 50	..		..	..	..	8 12	..
Machynlleth 146 (arr.	4 25 5 32	aft	7 58	..		..	..	..	8 16 8 25	..
(dep.	4 26 5 34	6 35	8 0	..		..	..	..	..	..
Dovey Junction ....arr.	4 33 5 40	6 41	8 6	..		..	..	..	..	..
146Towyn...........arr.	5 2 6 29	..	8744	..		..	..	..	8 54	..
146Barmouth ,,	5 32 6 59	..	9514	..		..	..	..	9 23	..
146Pwllheli ,,	7 8 8 40	..		..		..	..	..	..	..
Dovey Junction ....dep.	4 36 5 44	6 43	8 10	..		..	..	..	..	..
Glandyfi	.. 5 47	6 50	8 13	..		..	..	..	8 25	..
Ynyslas	.. 5 57	7 0		..		..	..	..	..	..
Borth	4 49 6 1	7 4	8 25	..		..	..	..	8 38	..
Llandre	.. 6 8	7 10	8 32	..		..	..	..	8 44	..
Bow Street	.. 6 12	7 14	8 36	..		..	..	..	8 48	..
Aberystwyth 141 .....arr.	5 5 6 30	7 23	8 45	..		..	..	..	8 57	..

A Sta nearly 2 mls from Montgomery.　B 1¼ mls from Cemmes.　B ¼ e . Liverpool (L. Stg.)12 20 & Birkenhead (W.) 12 23 aft. ,, Sats.　C Restaurant Car to Shrewsbury.　E Except Sats.　J Via Oswestry　N Restaurant Car to Wolverhampton.　S Sats. only.　T Tea Car to Wolverhampton　TC Thro Carriage.　U Arr Ellesmere 9 26 aft. x Dep. 4 10 ,, ,, Sats.　V Dep. 4 10 aft. Sats.　r Dep. 4 aft. on sats.　Xx Stops to set down from Shrewsbury or beyond on notice to Guard at Shrewsbury.　Y One cl. only.　Yy Calls at Montgomery and Cemmes Road to set down from Oswestry Shrewsbury, or beyond, on notice being given to Guard at Welshpool.　Z Sunday mrn.　s Saturday nights. ¶ 'Halt' at Plas-y-Court between Westbury & Breidden and at Commins Coch, between Llanbrynmair & Cemmes Road.

HISTORICAL BACKGROUND

The first line in the area was the Llanidloes & Newtown Railway, which opened on 2nd September 1859. It was followed by the Oswestry & Newtown Railway on 10th June 1861. Their Acts were passed in 1853 and 1855, respectively. The Newtown & Machynlleth Railway was authorised in 1857 and opened west to Borth on 5th January 1863. Completion to Aberystwyth was undertaken by the Aberystwyth & Welsh Coast Railway on 23rd June 1864 and all these lines became part of the new Cambrian Railways in 1864-65.

The Mawddwy Railway opened to all traffic on 1st October 1867 and was operated by the CR from 1911. The corresponding dates for the Van Railway were 1st December 1873 and 1896. It opened to freight on 14th August 1871. (The MR was closed between 1901 and 1911.)

The line west from Dovey Junction to Aberdovey opened in 1867 and the route south from Aberystwyth to Strata Florida came into use in the same year. The narrow gauge line from Aberystwyth to Devils Bridge was completed in 1902. All the routes mentioned became part of the Great Western Railway in 1922.

Another narrow gauge line was closely associated with the route from its opening until 1948. That was the Corris Railway, which is described in the Machynlleth section.

The Van line lost its passenger service in July 1879 and freight on 4th November 1940, also between 1893 and 1896, when the CR took the line over. The Dinas Mawddwy branch closed to passengers on 1st January 1931 and to freight on 1st July 1951. (It was closed completely between 8th April 1904 and 31st July 1911 - to passengers from 17th April 1901). The line south from Moat Lane Junction to Llanidloes closed to passengers in 1962 and freight in 1967.

With the advent of nationalisation, all lines in the area became part of the Western Region of British Railways on 1st January 1948. The route was transferred to the London Midland Region on 17th June 1963.

An important event in the history of the line took place in October 1988, when a Radio Electronic Token Block system was introduced, the control being at Machynlleth.

Privatisation resulted in Central Trains operating services from 2nd March 1997. However, after reorganisation in October 2001, Wales & Borders became the franchisee. Arriva Trains Wales took over in December 2003.

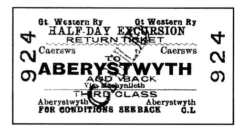

PASSENGER SERVICES

Throughout the CR era, timetables showed six weekday departures from Shrewsbury, with one or two more after 1910. Additionally, there were local trains originating at Whitchurch or Oswestry. On Sundays, there were two until the early 1880s and one thereafter.

The GWR takeover in 1922 brought few changes in the basic timetable. The Sunday train made few intermediate stops and ran from Oswestry.

The first BR timetable carried seven trains, all but two of which called at all stations and the Sunday one continued. Little changed with transfer of the route from the WR to the LMR in June 1963, but in June 1965 the Sunday service was withdrawn and six weekday departures from Shrewsbury became the norm again.

A similar frequency has been maintained subsequently, but with Sunday trains being run in the Summer only in most years.

For many years in the steam era, there were extra stopping trains between just Newtown and Machynlleth.

Van Branch

Initially there were two return journeys, with an extra one on Tuesdays. Later there were three, but only two on Saturdays. There were none on Sundays. With only six years of operation, there was little scope for change.

Dinas Mawddwy Branch

There were no Sunday trains; the number of weekday journeys varied from three to five. During much of the period of CR operation, two of the trains operated to and from Machynlleth, for the benefit of scholars.

July 1898   June 1869

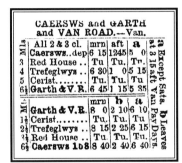

June 1883

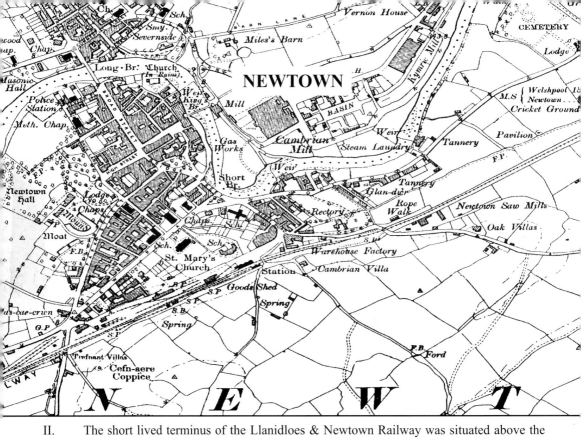

II.   The short lived terminus of the Llanidloes & Newtown Railway was situated above the word RAILWAY lower left on this 1903 map, which is scaled at 6ins to 1 mile. Winding across it is the River Severn and above this is BASIN. This was at the end of the 1821 Montgomeryshire Canal.

1.   This 1954 view is from the east and includes the goods shed and the unusually curved girders for the road bridge. The goods yard had a six-ton crane recorded in 1938 and during the 1930s there was a staffing level of 28 to 31. (Stations UK)

2. Built by BR, 2-6-4T no. 80131 calls with a down stopping train in 1962. The bay on the right was intended for trains to Brecon, but these mostly started at Moat Lane Junction in later years. The tall buildings are a reminder of the town's great involvement with the woollen industry. (A.M.Davies)

3. An April 1966 panorama records that gas lighting was still in favour, but town gas was soon discontinued. The platforms had recently been raised and resurfaced; little has changed since. (C.L.Caddy)

4. On the left is the "cow horn" and net for receiving single line tablets and on the right is the post for their despatch. These and the 35-lever box ceased to be used on 21st October 1988, when radio signalling from Machynlleth was introduced.
(Lens of Sutton coll.)

Newtown	1923	1933
Passenger tickets issued	58536	26712
Season tickets issued	73	65
Parcels forwarded	61329	51711
General goods forwarded (tons)	4681	3149
Coal and coke received (tons)	2266	4207
Other minerals received (tons)	3353	3232
General goods received (tons)	9492	7969
Trucks of livestock handled	513	344

5. The 15.45 Aberystwyth to Shrewsbury is approaching the station on 14th July 1966, as oil tankers stand at the end of the goods yard headshunt. The Cambrian Mountains are in the distance. Class 110 DMUs were introduced in 1957 and became common on the route in the early 1960s. (C.L.Caddy)

6. No. 37428 worked the Euston to Aberystwyth service on the Welsh part of the journey on 25th June 1988. The train ran on Summer Saturdays only and was first hauled by class 37s in 1985. (B.Robbins)

Other views of this station can be seen in our *Brecon to Newtown* and *Shrewsbury to Newtown* albums.

SCAFELL HALT

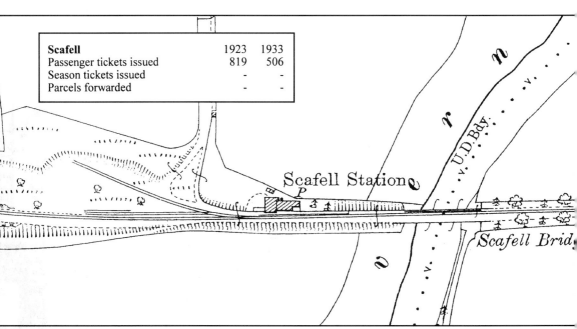

Scafell	1923	1933
Passenger tickets issued	819	506
Season tickets issued	-	-
Parcels forwarded	-	-

III.   The 1902 map has the River Severn on the right and a quarry siding on the left. This closed in May 1941, but was only used for wagon load traffic.

7.   The station was in use from May 1863 until July 1891. It reopened in July 1913, but double track had come into use on 26th July 1912 and so only an up platform was available. The halt closed in September 1954 and the line was singled in June 1965. It is seen between those dates, when in use as a dwelling. The total revenue had been £12 in 1923, dropping to £7 in 1938. (Lens of Sutton coll.)

MOAT LANE JUNCTION

8.   The station opened as Caersws and was renamed in January 1863 when Caersws was opened on the Cambrian line. The view east from the footbridge on 27th May 1958 includes the double track to Newtown and 2-6-0 no. 75005 taking water, which was supplied from the tank in the background. There was a staff of around 24 here for most of the 1930s. (G.Adams/M.J.Stretton coll.)

Moat Lane Junction	1923	1933
Passenger tickets issued	10471	4797
Season tickets issued	17	10
Parcels forwarded	194	287
General goods forwarded (tons)	310	88
Coal and coke received (tons)	29	47
Other minerals received (tons)	14	852
General goods received (tons)	20	40
Trucks of livestock handled	-	-

Other views can be seen in pictures 107-113 in *Brecon to Newtown.*

IV.   The 1902 map has the single line to Llanidloes at the bottom. This carried passengers until 31st December 1962 and limited freight until 2nd October 1967. The main line was single in 1902, but sidings are parallel to it on both sides of the map. Note that the station was only served by footpaths and that there are two footbridges drawn, but three annotated. West Box (left) had 15 levers and closed on 13th June 1965, when passing here ceased.

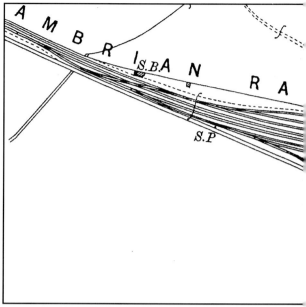

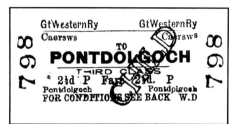

9.   No. 7818 *Granville Manor* can be admired westbound with the "Cambrian Coast Express" sometime in 1958. Most local goods traffic was handled at Caersws; the sidings here were mainly for transfer purposes. However, a peak in tonnage figures here in the later 1930s was probably due to the arrival of roadmaking material. (J.W.T.House/C.L.Caddy coll.)

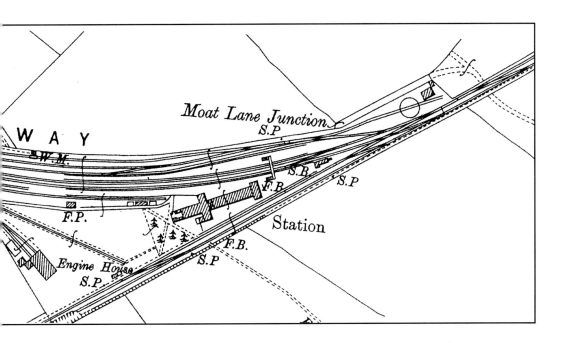

10.　No. 7819 *Hinton Manor* runs in with the 4.26pm arrival from Aberystwyth, while the 4.20 from Newtown to Machynlleth waits in the loop in August 1961. The exchange sidings are more evident in this view from the footbridge. The refreshment room had entrances from both adjacent platforms. (D.K.Jones coll.)

11.   The junction is seen from a westbound train and the straight line to Llanidloes is featured. The turntable site shown on the map had become an ash pit. Included is Moat Lane East Box which had a 53-lever frame from 1924 and closed on 13th June 1965. (A.M.Davies)

12.   The new turntable was 50ft in length and was situated in the V of the junction, west of the main building. An 0-6-0 is about to be turned to work a goods train to Oswestry on 31st March 1962. (J.Langford)

13.   A panorama from 26th May 1962 features no. 7803 *Barcote Manor* with the "Cambrian Coast Express" overtaking a local train. The former was due at 4.14pm and is probably running late; the latter was the 4.20 from Newtown, due away at 4.27, and had been sent on ahead. (A.M.Davies)

14.   The engine shed was damaged in a storm in 1955 and replaced in 1957 by the one seen here. It was photographed in May 1961 and closed on 31st December 1962, when the Brecon service was withdrawn. The station closed the same day. The wagons on the left are on the turntable road. (D.K.Jones coll.)

EAST OF CAERSWS

15.   As the line starts its final climb to the summit at Talerddig, it crosses the River Severn for the last time. A "Dukedog" class 4-4-0 is bound for Shrewsbury in August 1958. (P.Q.Treloar coll.)

Caersws	1923	1933
Passenger tickets issued	14816	9436
Season tickets issued	77	126
Parcels forwarded	4234	3186
General goods forwarded (tons)	297	231
Coal and coke received (tons)	311	509
Other minerals received (tons)	1762	1396
General goods received (tons)	1746	1085
Trucks of livestock handled	557	466

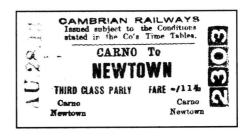

CAERSWS

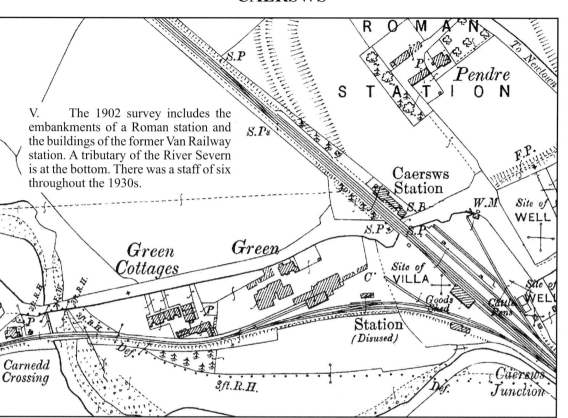

V.   The 1902 survey includes the embankments of a Roman station and the buildings of the former Van Railway station. A tributary of the River Severn is at the bottom. There was a staff of six throughout the 1930s.

16.   An Edwardian postcard reveals the extent of platform lengthening and shows a view unchanged in 2008, except that the wooden gates had been replaced by tubular steel ones. The signal box came into use on 15th June 1891. (Lens of Sutton coll.)

17.   Looking towards Moat Lane Junction in 1965, we see that the loop could accommodate two up trains. Beyond the signal box is the goods yard, which closed on 4th May 1964. (C.L.Caddy)

18.   Unusually for a station with a loop but only one platform, passenger trains could pass here, as seen on 17th June 1967. The 14.23 from Shrewsbury was the only down train scheduled not to call at Caersws, Mondays to Fridays. On the left is a class 101 and on the right a 103. (C.L.Caddy)

19.   Class 150 DMUs were recorded passing over the level crossing on 23rd June 1986. By that time, the signalman also sold tickets, but privatisation brought that to an end. The signals were still oil lit. (B.W.L.Brooksbank)

20.   No. 37418 was photographed on 28th April 1993, while working the final tanker train from Aberystwyth; it was destined for Stanlow refinery. Since 1988, when the loop was removed, the signaller had simply to open the gates by hand; this was still the case in 2008. (B.Robbins)

Van Branch

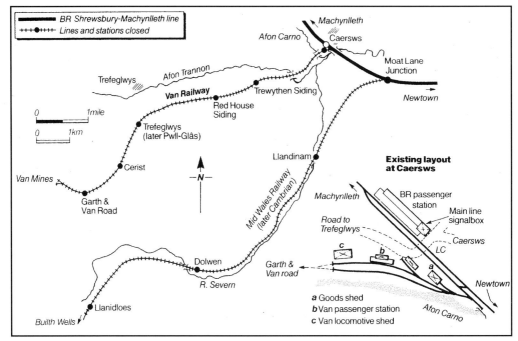

VI.   The railway was built to convey minerals from the lead mines at Van, but traffic declined owing to the import of better ores. After three years of closure, the CR operated the line on three days a week to convey waste stone for ballast, but this was poor quality. The GWR takeover brought horse traction west of Trefeglwys and total closure followed in 1940. Timber had been the main traffic at Cerist. (Railway Magazine)

21.   The Van Railway's terminus at Caersws was known as "Van Station" and the building on the right was the head office and was used by passengers, until their service ceased in 1879. In that year, fares generated £39 in total. On the left of this view from 1910 is the engine shed, last used as such in 1893, when the line first closed.(G.M.Perkins/R.S.Carpenter coll.)

22.   Seen in 1948, the GWR had improved the site and used it for its local Bridge Department, a purpose it served until 1984. The office was occupied in 1872-87 by John Ceiriog Hughes, who was VR general manager, but more widely known as a lyric poet and for providing words for "Men of Harlech". Agricultural engineers used the buildings at the start of the 21st century. (R.M.Casserley coll.)

TREFEGLWYS

23.   The VR bought two four-wheelers from the Midland Carriage & Wagon Co. Ltd, each with guards compartments. One was retained as a store at Trefeglwys and was photographed in the early 20th century, protected by its new custodian. The station house was still standing a century later. (G.M.Perkins/R.S.Carpenter coll.)

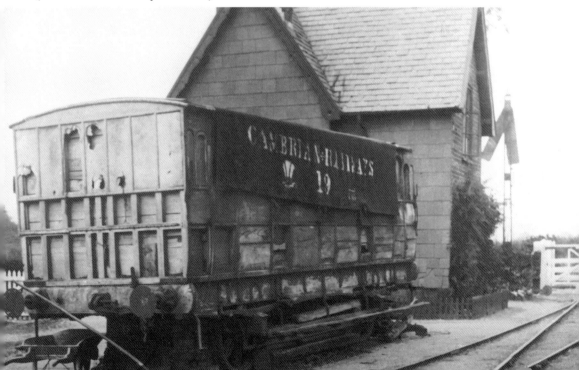

GARTH & VAN ROAD

24.   The VR's first loco was a Manning Wardle 0-6-0ST, this lasting until 1899 as CR no. 25. The second became no. 24 and was of a similar type, purchased in 1877. Seen at Van in around 1910 is no. 22, an 0-4-0ST from the same firm in 1901. (G.M.Perkins/R.S.Carpenter coll.)

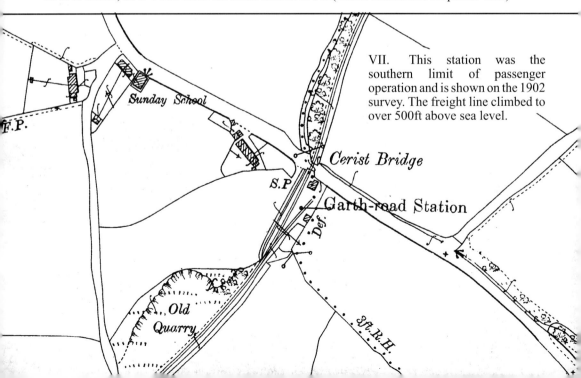

VII.   This station was the southern limit of passenger operation and is shown on the 1902 survey. The freight line climbed to over 500ft above sea level.

25.   This and the next picture are from 1948. Looking south we see the route of the mineral line in front of a terrace of 18 dwellings for miners. The best year for silver was 1876, with 59,000ozs produced. (R.S.Carpenter coll.)

26.   The Van mines were busy as early as 1850, but prosperity was intermittent, with many periods of closure and different ownership. Over 600 men were occupied in 1877, during one of the peaks, the number being down to 135 in 1913. The ground is severely poisoned and allows no weed growth. (R.S.Carpenter coll.)

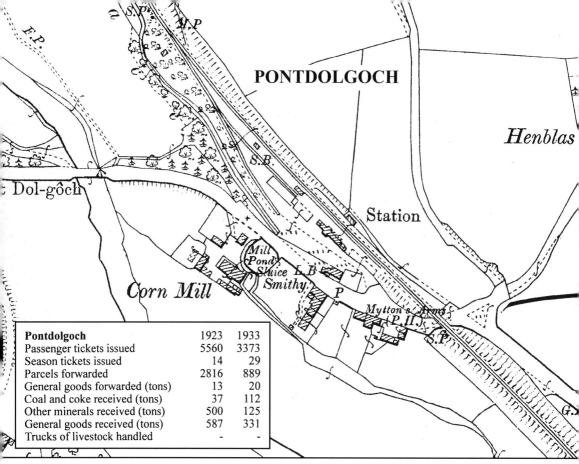

Pontdolgoch	1923	1933
Passenger tickets issued	5560	3373
Season tickets issued	14	29
Parcels forwarded	2816	889
General goods forwarded (tons)	13	20
Coal and coke received (tons)	37	112
Other minerals received (tons)	500	125
General goods received (tons)	587	331
Trucks of livestock handled	-	-

VIII.   The 1902 edition shows the spelling used locally and the main road passing under the line.

27.   An early postcard includes oil lighting and the signal box in the distance. This opened in 1891 and was closed by 1929. There was only one man employed here in the 1930s. (Lens of Sutton coll.)

28.   A train approaches the station in March 1962 and passes over the A470 at a great height, with the timber-framed inn on the left. Passenger service was withdrawn on 14th June 1965. (A.M.Davies)

29.   This is the scene one month after closure. To the left of the parcels shed was the goods yard, which had closed on 19th August 1963. Further west was Clatter Crossing, where there was a 24-lever signal box from 1914 to 1952. (C.L.Caddy)

CARNO

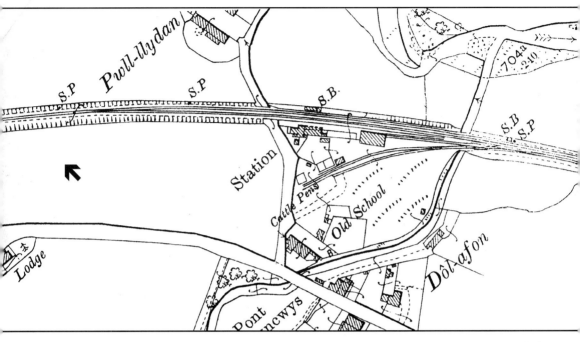

IX.   The 1902 edition indicates a stream passing under the tracks, near the signal box which was in the position shown from 1891 to 1928. The population fell from 717 in 1901 to 481 in 1961.

30.   An Aberystwyth to Whitchurch train is leaving Carno on 18th July 1938, hauled by no. 3211. This was earlier named *Earl of Ducie*. (P.Q.Treloar coll.)

31.   An undated panorama from the west end of the up platform reveals the generous dimensions of the goods shed. Rails did not pass through the west door, seen here. (M.J.Stretton coll.)

32.   No. 7820 *Dinmore Manor* was recorded on 25th July 1964. The signal box had 24 levers and there was a staff of four throughout the 1930s, this figure including signalmen. (A.M.Davies)

33.   Seen on the same day is 4-6-0 no. 75026. Freight facilities were withdrawn on 29th July 1963 and passenger service ended on 14th June 1965. (A.M.Davies)

→ 34. The fine stone building was still intact in 1986, although with the blemish of an aircon unit. The buildings had become part of the Laura Ashley factory complex, but this closed in 2005. The gates were similar to those at Caersws. (B.W.L.Brooksbank)

→ 35. No. 37428 is passing with the 15.40 Euston to Aberystwyth on 5th July 1986. The signal box closed on 21st October 1988, when automatic half barriers came into use. A station reopening campaign was underway in 2008. (B.Robbins)

Carno	1923	1933
Passenger tickets issued	7880	4551
Season tickets issued	18	51
Parcels forwarded	1753	1251
General goods forwarded (tons)	148	46
Coal and coke received (tons)	81	82
Other minerals received (tons)	316	747
General goods received (tons)	718	269
Trucks of livestock handled	55	25

Gt Western Ry.   Gt. Western Ry
TALERDDIG   TALERDDIG
TO
CARNO
THIRD CLASS
4d.   Fare   4d
Issued subject to the conditions&regulations set out in the Company's TimeTables, Bills & Notices
Carno   Carno

1334   1334

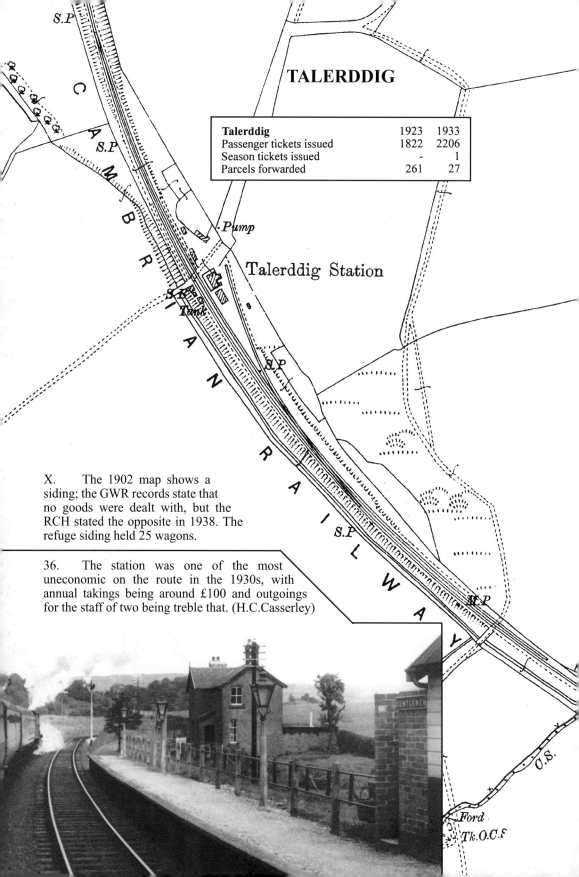

TALERDDIG

Talerddig	1923	1933
Passenger tickets issued	1822	2206
Season tickets issued	-	1
Parcels forwarded	261	27

Pump

Talerddig Station

X.   The 1902 map shows a
siding; the GWR records state that
no goods were dealt with, but the
RCH stated the opposite in 1938. The
refuge siding held 25 wagons.

36.   The station was one of the most
uneconomic on the route in the 1930s, with
annual takings being around £100 and outgoings
for the staff of two being treble that. (H.C.Casserley)

37.	The isolated spot near the summit was often cold and windswept. Snow lingers on 31st March 1962. Passenger trains ceased to call on 14th June 1965, but the loop was retained and was still in use in the 21st century. (J.Langford)

38.	Nos 37682 and 37684 head the 06.20 Birmingham New Street to Aberystwyth on 6th August 1988. The signal box had an 18-lever frame and was in use until 21st October of that year, having been built in about 1873. (B.Robbins)

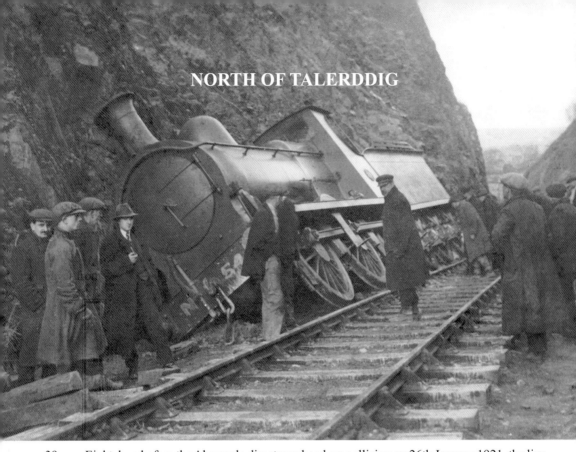

39.   Eight days before the Abermule disastrous head-on collision on 26th January 1921, the line was blocked in the steep-sided cutting below the station, where the gradient is 1 in 56 up from the coast. (R.M.Casserley coll.)

40.   The eastbound climb includes a severe test of 1 in 52 for two miles. Most goods trains were banked at the rear, while passenger trains had pilot engines. The assisting engine was removed at Talerddig station. Eight coaches was the usual limit for a lone "Manor" or BR class 4 4-6-0. No. 7803 *Barcote Manor* is climbing the bank on 30th May 1964. (E.Wilmshurst)

LLANBRYNMAIR

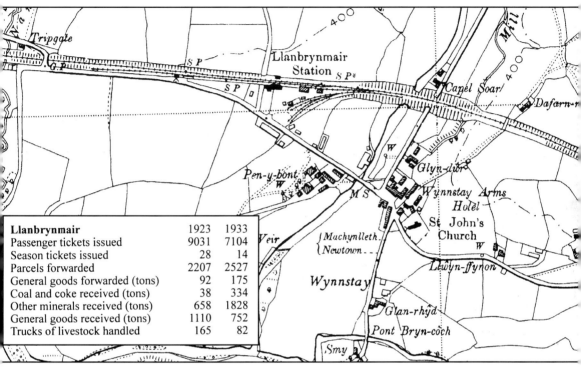

Llanbrynmair	1923	1933
Passenger tickets issued	9031	7104
Season tickets issued	28	14
Parcels forwarded	2207	2527
General goods forwarded (tons)	92	175
Coal and coke received (tons)	38	334
Other minerals received (tons)	658	1828
General goods received (tons)	1110	752
Trucks of livestock handled	165	82

XI.   The station is seen to be close to the village centre on this 1949 map at 12ins to 1 mile. The Z bend on the A470 is on the left.

41.   An early postcard features more fine barge boards and only half the staff, owing to shift work. The population was 1151 in 1901. The building was in good order in 2008 and used as a dwelling. (Lens of Sutton coll.)

42.　　The 9.45am Whitchurch to Aberystwyth runs in on 30th May 1964 behind 2-6-4T no. 80135. On the up platform is the small signal box. (E. Wilmshurst)

43.　　The up side was recorded on 23rd August 1954, along with the signal box, which had 11 levers and was in use from October 1890 to November 1966. The goods service was withdrawn on 4th May 1964 and passenger trains ceased to call on 14th June 1965. (H.C. Casserley)

COMMINS COCH HALT

44.   The halt opened on 19th October 1931 and closed on 14th June 1965. It is seen from a down train descending at 1 in 78. The brickwork on the right is on the top of an arch where the A470 passed *under* the railway after a much steeper descent. It now passes over the line. The mileage (68) was measured from Cambrian Junction, Whitchurch. (A.M.Davies)

45.   The platform was level with the main road (left) and served a small community. It is seen in May 1964. (C.L.Caddy)

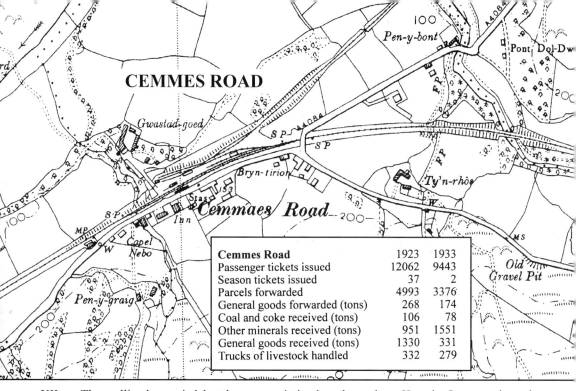

CEMMES ROAD

Cemmes Road	1923	1933
Passenger tickets issued	12062	9443
Season tickets issued	37	2
Parcels forwarded	4993	3376
General goods forwarded (tons)	268	174
Coal and coke received (tons)	106	78
Other minerals received (tons)	951	1551
General goods received (tons)	1330	331
Trucks of livestock handled	332	279

XII. The spelling has varied, but the pronunciation has always been Kem-is. Our route is on the right and the Dinas Mawddwy branch runs to the top from its own station. The map is from 1946 and is scaled at 12ins to 1 mile.

46. An eastbound train with a through bogie coach at the front was recorded on 2nd July 1907. Being oiled up before the stiff climb is 4-4-0 no. 64, which had been built by Sharp Stewart in 1893. (K.Nunn/LCGB coll.)

47. We now enter the beautiful Dovey Valley and the view includes the main road, the original low platforms, the cattle pens and stock on the branch line. (SLS coll.)

48. A panorama in the other direction features some fine finials, ornamental chimney pots, the roofless accommodation for gentlemen and contrasting styles of barge board. The goods shed (centre) was in use until the yard closed on 4th May 1964. (R.M.Casserley coll.)

49. The freight for the branch approaches on 27th April 1950 behind 0-4-2T no. 1434. We are looking from the signal box, which had a 25-lever frame. It could work the catch point, which was provided owing to the 1 in 163 gradient. (W.A.Camwell/SLS coll.)

50.   Accelerating westwards is 4-6-0 no. 7827 *Lydham Manor*. (It was running on the Paignton & Dartmouth Steam Railway in 2008.) Passenger trains ceased to stop here after 14th June 1965. (A.M.Davies)

51.   The signal box was photographed on 23rd June 1986, along with the main station building. The former closed on 11th March 1984 and was dismantled for use on the Dean Forest Railway. The loop lasted until that time. The road is on the branch alignment. (B.W.L.Brooksbank)

Dinas Mawddwy Branch
CEMMES ROAD

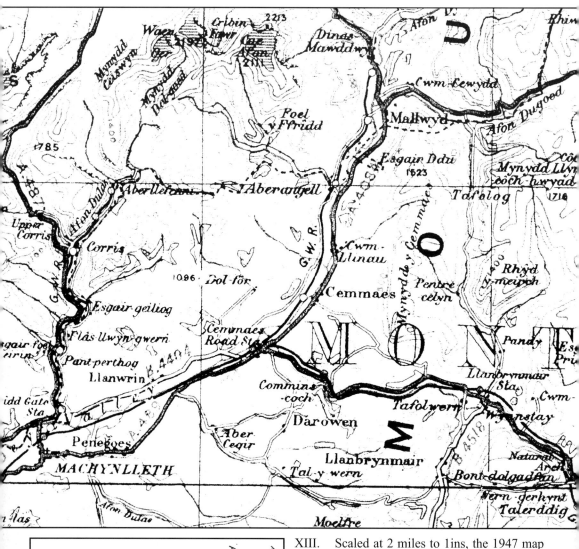

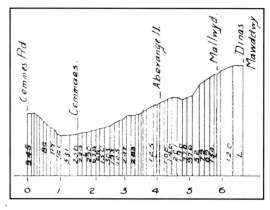

XIII.   Scaled at 2 miles to 1ins, the 1947 map shows closed stations with clear circles. It also includes the Corris Railway, on the left.

Branch gradient profile.

52.   The leading coach (no. 4) has two second class compartments with a first in the centre, while the other one (no. 5) is all third. Both were ex-LNWR. *Mawddwy* was new from Manning Wardle in 1867; a similar engine came from the same builder in 1868 and was named *Disraeli*. (P.Q.Treloar coll.)

53.   The fortune of the Mawddwy Railway was closely related to that of the local landowner who had promoted it, along with some local businesses. This platform was not used in 1901-11. Buses began to run in 1924 and no branch platforms were used after 1930. Near the locomotive is the gable end of the goods shed seen in picture no. 48. (R.S.Carpenter coll.)

CEMMAES

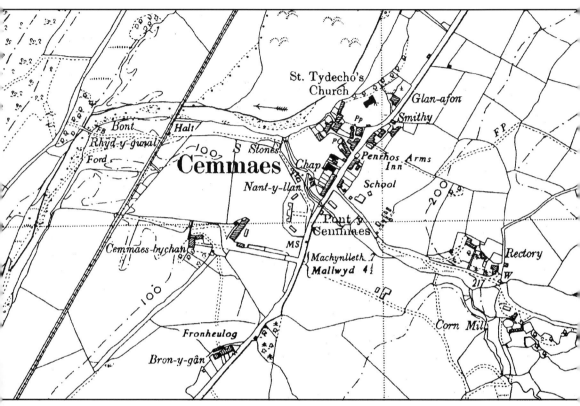

XIV.   The population in 1901 was 722; this survey at 12ins to 1 mile is from that period, but it does not show a siding. A footpath reaches the halt and then passes over the Dovey on a bridge.

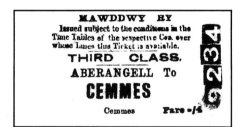

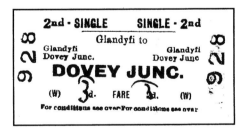

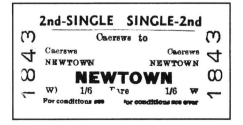

54.   This photograph is from July 1904. During the total closure period, the mail was pushed on a trolley by a fireman. (SLS coll.)

55.   A northward view from 1948 shows the halt beyond two bridges. This differs from the map and we presume that the alterations were made after its publication. (R.S.Carpenter coll.)

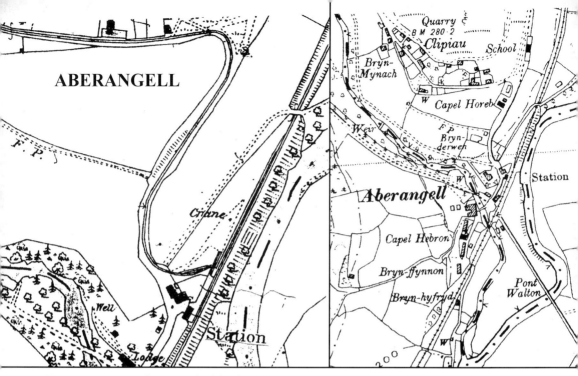

XVa. A tramway from Hendreddu Slate Quarry ran to the station from 1876 and around 200 tons of slab and slates were conveyed each month. The line came along the lane top left and ran down to the wharf, shown on the 1st edition at 25 miles to 1 ins. The right part is at 12 ins to 1 mile and is from 1946.

56. A 1904 image includes the station building and a cottage; both are shown on the map to be south of the loop. (R.M.Casserley coll.)

57. Looking north in 1948, we see the five-ton crane which handled much timber traffic. There had usually been three goods trains per week since 1930. (R.S.Carpenter coll.)

MALLWYD

XVb. 1902 map

58. A southward view from 1948 shows the remains of a station which served a community of 885 in 1901. This was in steady decline, as was the track. (R.S.Carpenter coll.)

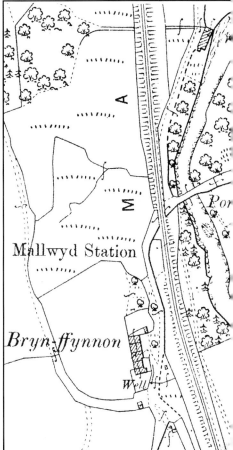

DINAS MAWDDWY

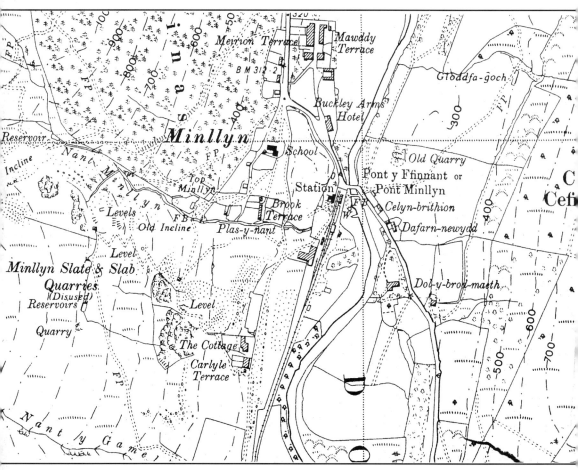

XVI.   The quarries are about 400ft above the station, which is shown on this 1949 map at 12ins to 1 mile. The main road has since been straightened.

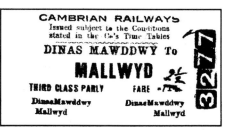

59.   There were six different secondhand coaches in use on the MR, but two normally sufficed. This postcard has the goods shed on the right. (SLS coll.)

60.   This record from August 1939 includes the engine shed (left). It was used until the end of 1930, when passenger service ceased. The shed on the right had replaced the one seen in the previous photograph. (W.A.Camwell/SLS coll.)

61.   This imposing gateway also appears in picture 59. This and the next two pictures date from 23rd September 1948, when the terminus was in terminal decline. The GWR had placed a camp coach here in the 1930s. (W.A.Camwell/SLS coll.)

➔ 62. No. 1434 waits to return to Machynlleth; the three railway buildings are on the right. Partially concealed by the wagons is the Meirion Mill complex, which was centered on a slate mill; it included an ammunition store during World War I and a timber mill subsequently. In 1946, it became a woollen mill, spinning local wool. (W.A.Camwell/SLS coll.)

➔   63. A closer look at the main building reveals a small bay window from which the station master could keep his domain under surveillance. The track was considered dangerous by some in 1948. (W.A.Camwell/SLS coll.)

64.   A new owner in 1966 improved all the buildings and introduced weaving to the mill. As an added visitor attraction, a 2ft gauge railway was laid alongside and an early Alan Keef loco arrived from the National Centre for Alternative Technology in 1975. The 0-4-0ST *Trixie* is seen near the old engine shed that year, but the line closed in about 1979 and the engine went to Belgium. The diesel *Tadpole* went to Cumberland. (A.M.Davies)

65.   Weaving and manufacture ceased, but woollen products and good catering continue to be on offer. The old gateway and building were photographed in September 1999. (B.W.L.Brooksbank)

MACHYNLLETH

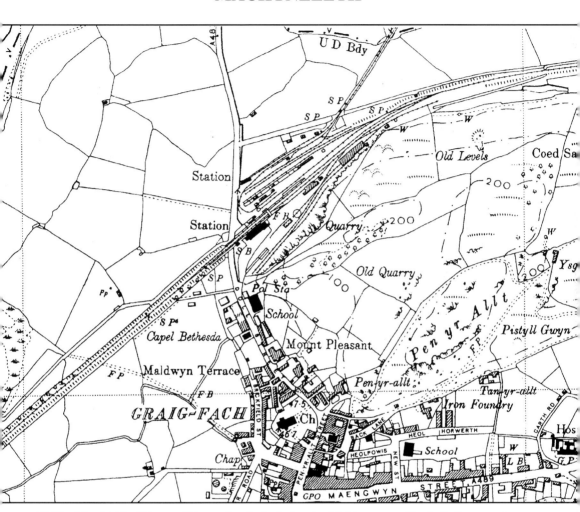

XVII. The 1948 edition at 12ins to 1 mile includes the 2ft 3ins gauge Corris Railway at the top; it closed that year, having lost its passenger service in 1930. It had originally run (from 1859) a further 2½ miles west to wharves on the Dovey at Derwenlas, but this section was lost under the new main line in 1863.

Machynlleth	1923	1933
Passenger tickets issued	37535	27079
Season tickets issued	78	113
Parcels forwarded	20340	23590
General goods forwarded (tons)	2848	3675
Coal and coke received (tons)	1347	1063
Other minerals received (tons)	1805	5214
General goods received (tons)	4486	4954
Trucks of livestock handled	474	443

CAMBRIAN RAILWAYS
Issued subject to the Conditions
stated in the Company's Time Tables

MACHYNLLETH To
ABERYSTWYTH

THIRD CLASS PARLY   FARE 1/8½
Machynlleth   Machynlleth
Aberystwyth   Aberystwyth

9429

66.　　A panorama from the bridge over the main road includes a sign TO THE CORRIS RAILWAY STATION and the East signal box in the distance. It had a 23-lever frame and was in use from 27th August 1890 until 27th March 1960. No. 43 *Plynlimmon* was a 2-4-0, new from Sharp Stewart in 1864. (Lens of Sutton coll.)

67.　　A 1948 view includes West Box, which had 13 levers and was in use in the same period as East. The up platform had been raised in 1937 and a new waiting shelter provided. The station is still gas lit; BR brought over 600 tons of coal for the gasworks in 1949. It was in production from 1865 to 1962. (H.C.Casserley)

68.   Seen in 1956, the impressive structure had some notable chimney stacks. It supported a staff of 39 in 1923, this figure including train crews. The population of the town fell from 2038 in 1901 to 1840 in 1961. (H.C.Casserley)

69.   Two fine panoramas from 1965 set the scene. On the edge of the wide Dovey Valley are the terminal buildings of the Corris Railway and also Lower Yard, which handled general goods. The white flat roof is on the 50-lever signal box, which superseded the earlier two. Behind it is the six-ton crane. (C.C.Green/G.Williams coll.)

70.   On the right is the coal stage and to the left of it is the new goods shed; it largely obscures the signal box. The turntable was 55ft in length; there was also a 50ft one to the right of the engine shed in the distance. (C.C.Green/G.Williams coll.)

71.   The three-road part of the engine shed dated from 1873 and the two-road section beyond was built in 1863. They were photographed in July 1966, as steam was coming to an end. (R.Ruffell/M.J.Stretton coll.)

72.   The 12.28 to Aberystwyth on 12th August 1989 was formed of a class 150 DMU, unpopular because of their noise. Class 153s, 156s and 158s followed. (T.Heavyside)

73.   The west end of the yard was photographed on 7th June 2003. The main station building was used by Mid Wales Tourism at that time. (M.J.Stretton)

74.   The joining and dividing of trains had become a welcome improvement in coastal service in recent years. Seen from the footbridge on 1st September 2008 are two coaches from Pwllheli awaiting coaches to form the 12.02 to Birmingham New Street. On the right is the Machynlleth Train Care Facility, which was opened on 13th August 2007. In the distance is the original engine shed, which had been reroofed to serve an area used for refuelling and underfloor cleaning. There were 24 employees at that period. (V.Mitchell)

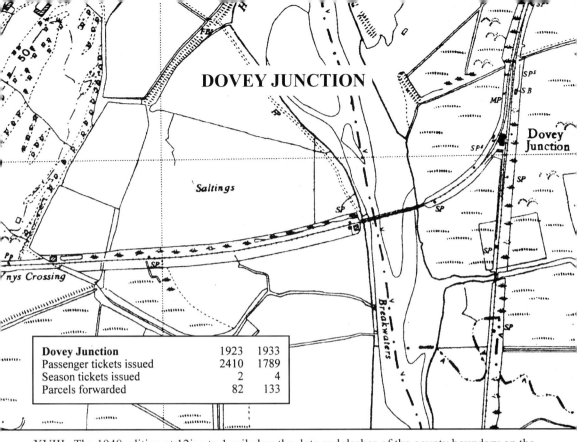

DOVEY JUNCTION

Saltings

'nys Crossing

Dovey
Junction

Breakwaters

Dovey Junction	1923	1933
Passenger tickets issued	2410	1789
Season tickets issued	2	4
Parcels forwarded	82	133

XVIII. The 1948 edition at 12ins to 1 mile has the dots and dashes of the county boundary on the deepest part of the river and the station masters house is on the left, at Ynys Crossing. Note that there was no public access to the station at that time. Three counties join lower right.

75.   The extensive marshland is evident as a train waits to depart for Pwllheli in the 1930s. The locomotive is GWR 2-4-0 no. 3225. The booking office was closed from 1902 to 1916 to prevent trespass. A path was then provided across the bridge for pass holders, but women and children were not allowed on it. (R.S.Carpenter coll.)

76.   A 1948 view in the other direction is from a London train and features the widening estuary. Other departure boards stand near the base of the post. The refreshment room had been created in 1881. There was a staff of six for most of the 1930s. (H.C.Casserley)

→ 77. Opened as Glandovey Junction on 29th June 1890, this 52-lever box was renamed Dovey Junction in 1904, along with the station. The box is seen in 1948 and was in use until 22nd February 1959. (H.C.Casserley)

↓ 78. The replacement signal box is in this and the next two pictures. The two portions of the up "Cambrian Coast Express" are being joined and 4-6-0 no. 75014 stands, while another engine blows off on 12th June 1965. The line on the far left is the through loop; it had no platform. (T.J.Edgington)

79.   A Derby-built DMU is bound for Pwllheli on 27th June 1966, during high tide. The box on the right had a 65-lever frame and functioned until 22nd October 1988. Thereafter there was only a single point and it was positioned well north of the platforms, so that its motor was above flood level. (T.J.Edgington)

80.   The replacement station buildings from 1956 are evident on 25th June 1981 as the 10.07 Aberystwyth to Shrewsbury approaches. Waiting in the loop is the 08.55 from Shrewsbury. (T.Heavyside)

81.   Steam returned on 2nd August 1987 and no. 7819 *Hinton Manor* is seen with the second run of the day to Aberystwyth. The loop on the right was replaced 21 years later. (H.Ballantyne)

82.   Only a simple shelter was to be seen on 1st September 2008. The platforms and tracks were being raised up to 2ft to reduce flooding. (V.Mitchell)

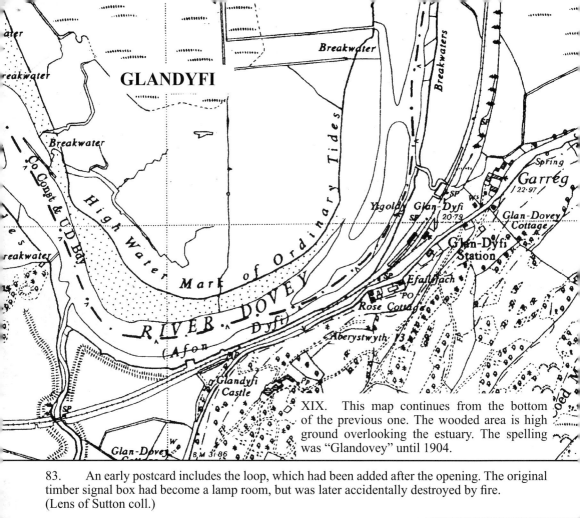

GLANDYFI

XIX.   This map continues from the bottom of the previous one. The wooded area is high ground overlooking the estuary. The spelling was "Glandovey" until 1904.

83.   An early postcard includes the loop, which had been added after the opening. The original timber signal box had become a lamp room, but was later accidentally destroyed by fire. (Lens of Sutton coll.)

84.   A later postcard includes a section of wooden platform, which was provided owing to the softness of the ground. The firm material descends steeply on the right. (SLS coll.)

85.   The down "Cambrian Coast Express" passes an up local train on 2nd June 1962. Featured is 4-6-0 no. 7823 *Hook Norton Manor* and a camp coach. (B.W.L.Brooksbank)

86.   We look west in 1963; passenger service ceased here on 14th June 1965. The staff numbered two from 1931 to 1938. (C.C.Green/G.Williams coll.)

Glandyfi	1923	1933
Passenger tickets issued	7775	3154
Season tickets issued	28	17
Parcels forwarded	1844	2748
General goods forwarded (tons)	411	26
Coal and coke received (tons)	162	170
Other minerals received (tons)	146	566
General goods received (tons)	374	367
Trucks of livestock handled	19	11

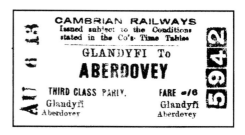

87.   The signal box was opened on 23rd February 1891 and was fitted with a frame containing 17 levers. It is seen in 1963 and closed on 4th November 1973, when the loop was lost. (C.C.Green/G.Williams coll.)

88.   The goods yard is seen at about the time of its closure on 19th August 1963. The weigh bridge has been provided secondhand by the GWR in 1924. (C.C.Green/G.Williams coll.)

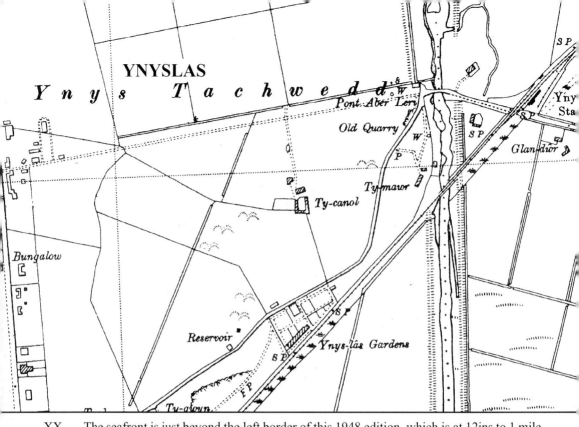

XX.   The seafront is just beyond the left border of this 1948 edition, which is at 12ins to 1 mile. The station opened on 1st July 1863.

89.   Our photographic survey is mainly from 1963. The down platform was unusual in retaining its original height at the south end. Short trains stopped at the higher part. On the right is the crossing gate lock lever. (C.C.Green/G.Williams coll.)

90.   The goods yard closed on 19th August 1963. The cattle pen is on the right and the porch is on the house, which was occupied by a station mistress for many years. There were three employees listed in the 1930s. (C.C.Green/G.Williams coll.)

Ynyslas	1923	1933
Passenger tickets issued	6073	1586
Season tickets issued	10	25
Parcels forwarded	905	317
General goods forwarded (tons)	33	1
Coal and coke received (tons)	5	13
Other minerals received (tons)	266	225
General goods received (tons)	238	74
Trucks of livestock handled	28	16

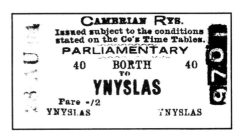

91.   Fierce winds can be damaging at this exposed location, thus the signal box lost many of its slates during a storm; hence the tarpaulin for its final months. There had been a siding curving away westwards to East Mill until April 1896. The Aberdovey Ferry Branch lasted only to 1867 and no trace remains. (C.C.Green/G.Williams coll.)

92.   The loop was taken out of use on 7th September 1963 and the signal box closed one week later. It had opened in 1896 and had 17 levers. Parcels service was withdrawn in 1938. (C.C.Green/G.Williams coll.)

93.   Passenger service ceased on 14th June 1965 and the photograph was taken a month later.
The main building was started in 1873, but it sank so fast that the upper storey was soon removed
to reduce its weight. The sand dunes are on the right. (C.L.Caddy)

CAMBRIAN RAILWAYS
Issued subject to the conditions
stated on the Co's Time Tables.
BORTH To
BOW STREET
THIRD CLASS (PARLY) FARE -7½
Borth   Borth
BowStreet   BowStreet

CAMBRIAN RAILWAYS
Issued subject to the conditions
stated in the Co's Time Tables.
LLANFIHANGEL To
BORTH
THIRD CLASS PARLY   FARE ·12½
Llanfihangel   Llanfihangel
Borth   Borth

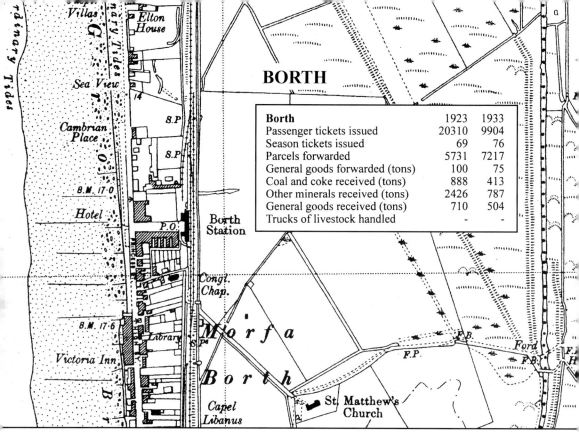

BORTH

Borth	1923	1933
Passenger tickets issued	20310	9904
Season tickets issued	69	76
Parcels forwarded	5731	7217
General goods forwarded (tons)	100	75
Coal and coke received (tons)	888	413
Other minerals received (tons)	2426	787
General goods received (tons)	710	504
Trucks of livestock handled	-	-

XXI. The station was a terminus for a little over 12 months in 1863-64. Borth was a seafront development with marshy ground inland. The 1948 map is at 12ins to 1 mile. The population was 861 in 1961.

94.   A down platform was added in 1894 and lengthened in 1911. A footbridge arrived in 1900 and was replaced by this concrete one in 1954. The camp coach was situated close to the beach and local facilities. (C.C.Green/G.Williams coll.)

95.   A southward panorama has the marshland on the left, together with the refuge siding, which could take 38 wagons. This and the next two pictures were taken in 1963. Five were employed here in the thirties. (C.C.Green/G.Williams coll.)

96.		The area was developed by one of the CR directors and the spacious Cambrian Terrace had the station building at its east end. The bowling green was on the left. (C.C.Green/G.Williams coll.)

97.		A chapel is in the background as no. 3200 runs in with a pick-up goods. Electric lighting replaced oil in 1936. The goods yard closed on 1st June 1964. (G.Coltas/Ted Hancock coll.)

98.   The 17-lever signal box of 1891 is included in this 1966 northward view. It was closed on 4th November 1973 and the loop was taken out of use at that time. (H.C.Casserley)

99.   The GWR replaced the original delicate canopy with this one in about 1930. No. M50208 is leading the 11.45 from Aberystwyth on 25th June 1981. Little had changed when the structures were adopted as part of a community partnership scheme in March 2006. Further south was Capel Soar level crossing which received automatic lights in January 1989. (T.Heavyside)

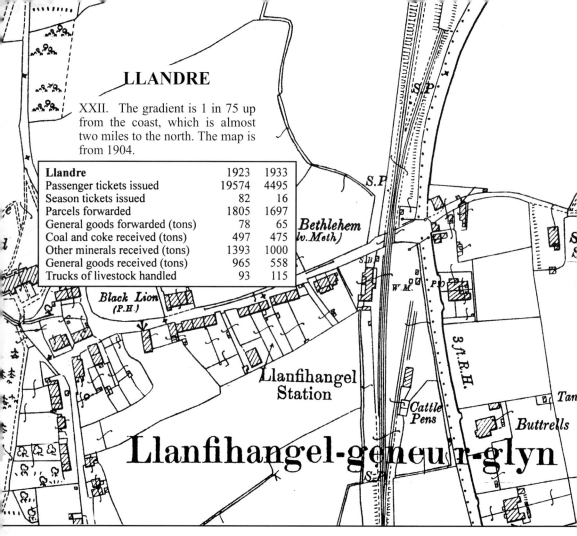

LLANDRE

XXII. The gradient is 1 in 75 up from the coast, which is almost two miles to the north. The map is from 1904.

Llandre	1923	1933
Passenger tickets issued	19574	4495
Season tickets issued	82	16
Parcels forwarded	1805	1697
General goods forwarded (tons)	78	65
Coal and coke received (tons)	497	475
Other minerals received (tons)	1393	1000
General goods received (tons)	965	558
Trucks of livestock handled	93	115

100.   The name was Llanfihangel until 1st August 1916. We first have four photographs from 1963 and begin by looking north. (C.C.Green/G.Williams coll.)

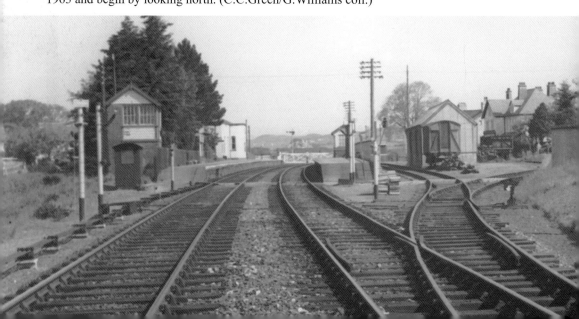

101.   Each gate had to be moved by hand. The wharf siding site for the Hafan Tramway was behind the camera. It was used for lead ore from 1893 to 1899 and lifted in 1911. A passenger service was provided briefly, in 1897-98. The gates were replaced by automatic lights on 26th January 1989. (C.C.Green/G.Williams coll.)

102.   On the left is the weigh house and beyond it is the 1883 goods shed. There had once been a 5-ton crane, but it collapsed and a timber loader died of his injuries. The goods yard closed on 1st June 1964. (C.C.Green/G.Williams coll.)

103.   The first signal box had been on the right, hence the rodding tunnel. The down platform was added in 1911, but canopies were never provided. There were four men on the payroll in the 1930s. (C.C.Green/G.Williams coll.)

104.   The signal box had 16 levers and was functional from 1911 until November 1966. Photographed in July 1965 is a class 108 DMU at speed. The station had closed to passengers on 14th June of that year. (C.L.Caddy)

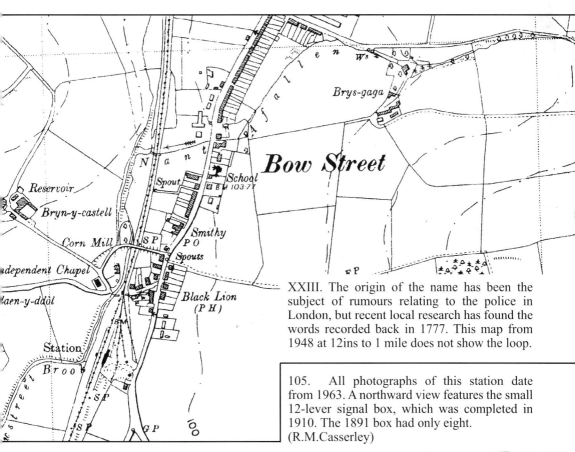

XXIII. The origin of the name has been the subject of rumours relating to the police in London, but recent local research has found the words recorded back in 1777. This map from 1948 at 12ins to 1 mile does not show the loop.

105. All photographs of this station date from 1963. A northward view features the small 12-lever signal box, which was completed in 1910. The 1891 box had only eight. (R.M.Casserley)

106.   The staff level was three for many decades. The 10.40am Aberystwyth to Oswestry freight is hauled by no. 7828 *Odney Manor*. (C.C.Green/G.Williams coll.)

Bow Street	1923	1933
Passenger tickets issued	23034	4808
Season tickets issued	45	18
Parcels forwarded	908	1560
General goods forwarded (tons)	1464	177
Coal and coke received (tons)	476	516
Other minerals received (tons)	477	923
General goods received (tons)	410	187
Trucks of livestock handled	5	12

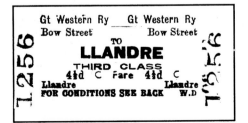

107.   The cement silo was erected in connection with the building of Nant-y-Moch Reservoir. The goods yard was closed on 1st June 1964. The approach to the station is on the right. (C.C.Green/G.Williams coll.)

108.   The local landowner had demanded a superior and more impressive station than the standard pattern on the route. Picture 106 includes a bay window. Passenger service ceased here on 14th June 1965. (C.C.Green/G.Williams coll.)

109.   The train seen in picture 106 is on the left now and on the right is no. 7820 *Dinmore Manor*. Both locomotives were preserved and both were running on the West Somerset Railway in 2008. (C.C.Green/G.Williams coll.)

NORTH OF ABERYSTWYTH

110.   The final mile of the route was doubled in 1924 and Llanbadarn Crossing box was opened; it contained a 12-lever frame. It is seen on 26th June 1970 and it closed upon line singling on 14th April 1983. Llanbadarn station was on the Vale of Rheidol two-foot gauge line and was immediately to the south. (C.L.Caddy)

111.   The town had its first gasworks in 1839, but a siding was laid at Plascrug Fields, Morfa Road, for a new one in 1898. It opened in 1902 and is seen from the VoR line shortly after gas production ceased in 1962. There was an unusual facing siding off the up line and coal was propelled from the terminus to it. Tonnage of coal delivered was 4654 in 1913 and over 10,000 in 1949. (C.C.Green/G.Williams coll.)

CAMBRIAN COAST EXPRESS

LONDON (Paddington), ABERDOVEY, TOWYN, BARMOUTH and ABERYSTWYTH

WEEK DAYS

		R E	R S				R S	R E
		am	am				am	am
London (Paddington) ..dep		10A10	10A50	Aberystwyth .. ..dep			9A25	11A15
			pm	Borth .. .. ,,			9A45	11A38
Banbury General	{arr	11 22	12 11	Dovey Junction .. ..arr			10 0	11 57
	{dep	11 23	12 14					
Leamington Spa	{arr	..	12 39	Barmouth.. .. ..dep			..	11A0
General	{dep	..	12 42	Barmouth Junction.. ,,			8A45	11A5
		pm		Fairbourne .. .. ,,			8A50	11A9
Birmingham	{arr	12 10	1 16	Llwyngwril .. .. ,,			9A5	11A20
(Snow Hill)	{dep	12 14	1 19	Tonfanau .. .. .. ,,			9 15	11 28
Wolverhampton	{arr	12 33	1 39	Towyn .. .. .. ,,			9A22	11A33
(Low Level)	{dep	12 40	1 45	Aberdovey .. .. ,,			9A31	11A40
Shrewsbury	{arr	1 17	..	Penhelig Halt .. .. ,,			9 36	11 43
	{dep	1 23	..	Dovey Junction ..arr			9 50	11 56
Welshpool .. .. ..arr		2 0	2 56					
Newtown .. .. .. ,,		2 28	3 26					
Machynlleth .. .. ,,		3 15	4 18	Dovey Junction .. ..dep			10A8	pm 12A5
				Machynlleth .. .. .. ,,			10A20	12A16
Machynlleth .. ..dep		3 40	4 30	Newtown .. .. .. ,,			11 17	1 24
Penhelig Halt .. ..arr		4 4	4 51	Welshpool .. .. .. ,,			11 55	1 55
Aberdovey .. .. ,,		4 10	4 56	Shrewsbury	{arr		..	2 33
Towyn .. .. .. ,,		4 17	5 3		{dep		..	2 40
Llwyngwril .. .. ,,		4 34	5 15			pm		
Fairbourne .. .. ,,		4 42	5 23	Wolverhampton	{arr	1 11		3 28
Barmouth Junction.. ,,		4 45	5 25	(Low Level) ..	{dep	1 16		3 33
Barmouth .. .. ,,		4 51	5 31	Birmingham	{arr	1 38		3 55
				(Snow Hill)	{dep	1 41		4 0
Machynlleth .. ..dep		3 20	4 23	Leamington Spa	{arr	2 11		4 23
Borth .. ..arr		3 45	4 46	General	{dep	2 12		4 24
Aberystwyth .. .. ,,		4 5	5 10	London (Paddington) ..arr		4 10		6 0

A—Seats can be reserved in advance on payment of a fee of 1s. 0d. per seat

E—Except Saturdays.

R—Refreshment Car facilities to and from Aberystwyth.

S—Saturdays only.

XXIV. June to September 1955.

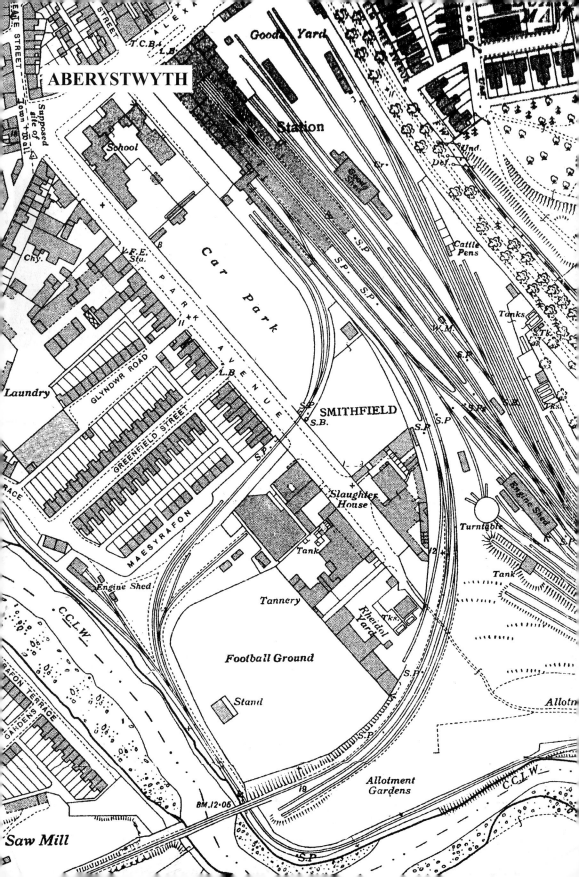

ABERYSTWYTH

STREET

ALEXA

T.C.B.

L.B.

Goods Yard

Station

School

Supposed
site of
Town Wall

Chy.

V.F.E.
Sta.

B

PARK

Car Park

AVENUE

Laundry

GLYNDWR ROAD

L.B.

GREENFIELD STREET

SMITHFIELD

S.B.

S.P.

MAESYRAFON

RACE

SP

Slaughter
House

Tank

Engine Shed

C.C.L.W.

Tannery

Rheidal
Yard

Tks.

RAFON TERRACE

GARDENS

Football Ground

Stand

Cr.

Und.

Del.

Cattle
Pens

Tanks

W.M.

S.P.

S.P.

S.P.

S.P.

S.P.

S.P.

Tks.

Turntable

Engine Shed

Tank

V2

S.P.

S.P.

Allotn

Allotment
Gardens

C.C.L.W.

BM.12·06

19

S.P.

Saw Mill

S.P.

112.   Waiting to leave on 5th June 1920 is an ex-Metropolitan Railway 4-4-0T, numbered 34 by the CR. There had earlier been four tracks between the platforms, but nos 3 and 4 (left) had been widened. Nos 4 and 5 were used for Carmarthen trains on the Manchester & Milford Haven line. (K.Nunn/LCGB)

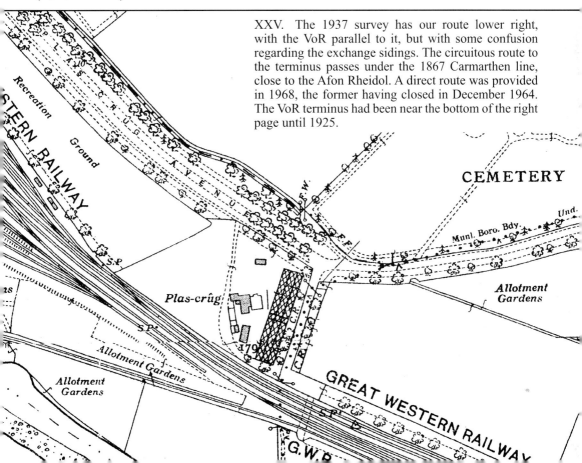

XXV. The 1937 survey has our route lower right, with the VoR parallel to it, but with some confusion regarding the exchange sidings. The circuitous route to the terminus passes under the 1867 Carmarthen line, close to the Afon Rheidol. A direct route was provided in 1968, the former having closed in December 1964. The VoR terminus had been near the bottom of the right page until 1925.

CEMETERY

Munl. Boro. Bdy.

Und.

Allotment Gardens

Recreation Ground

Plas-crûg

Allotment Gardens

Allotment Gardens

GREAT WESTERN RAILWAY

G.W.R.

113.   The 1906 shed was replaced in 1938-39 by one at a higher level and a turning triangle was completed in 1940. The frame carried a hoist used for rewheeling locomotives. There was a total staff of around 60 in the 1930s. (J.Moss/R.S.Carpenter coll.)

114.   The GWR takeover of the CR resulted in plans being soon drawn up for this neo-Georgian style structure, which was completed in 1926. The first floor "Assembly Room" served as a restaurant and on weekday afternoons offered "Thé Dansant", with a small orchestra. In 1935 it was converted to the GPO telephone exchange. The photograph is from 1962, as are the next two. (C.C.Green/G.Williams coll.)

→ 115. The concourse was spacious and well lit, generous facilities being provided all round. By 2008, the area had been encroached upon by catering facilities for the benefit of King Cash.
(C.C.Green/G.Williams coll.)

Aberystwyth	1913	1923	1933
Passenger tickets issued	40269	175936	96580
Season tickets issued	*	95	585
Parcels forwarded	22450	82452	117259
General goods forwarded (tons)	2321	3092	2914
Coal and coke received (tons)	1407	5630	6741
Other minerals received (tons)	1017	8862	9497
General goods received (tons)	3031	16156	18469
Trucks of livestock handled	6184	44679	41532
(* not available)			

→   116. A panorama from the upper storey includes the former stable block, top left. An ex-Army Bedford lorry loads coal near a Morris Minor van. Coal traffic continued until 1983 and oil until 1993. The yard was provided with a 6-ton crane in 1930; it is to the left of the goods shed, which is top right.
(C.C.Green/G.Williams coll.)

117. The platform numbers were reversed and so D7080 waits with a Carmarthen train at No. 3 and at No. 5 is no. 7822 *Foxcote Manor*. The date is 29th May 1964. (C.L.Caddy)

118. Seen on the same day from the east is the coal stage of the usual GWR type, under a large water tank. The shed was coded 89C and closed on 10th April 1965. It reopened for VoR locos on 20th May 1968. On the right is the 1924 signal box, which had 100 levers and closed on 25th April 1982, as did the goods yard. The platforms are in the right background. (C.L.Caddy)

119.   A return excursion to Birmingham was recorded on 25th June 1981, with nos 25073 and 25219 in charge. VoR tracks had been laid between the Carmarthen platforms and one of the coaches is evident on the left. (T.Heavyside)

120.   The first DMU had arrived here on 8th September 1957 and classes 153 and 156 were to be seen on 11th August 1992 forming the 11.00 to Birmingham New Street. Only two ground frames remained, these controlling a little used loop. On offer at the start of the 21st century was a smart station offering two ticket offices, a choice of buffets and even a choice of track gauges. (P.G.Barnes)

MIDDLETON PRESS
EVOLVING THE ULTIMATE RAIL ENCYCLOPEDIA

Easebourne Lane, Midhurst, West Sussex.
GU29 9AZ   Tel:01730 813169

www.middletonpress.co.uk   email:info@middletonpress.co.uk
A-978 0 906520 B-978 1 873793 C-978 1 901706 D-978 1 904474 E-978 1 906008

OOP Out of print at time of printing - Please check availability   BROCHURE AVAILABLE SHOWING NEW TITLES